TAME TURTLE

Connect the dots from **1** to **5**.
Color the picture.

PICNIC ANTICS

Connect the dots from **1** to **5**.
Color the picture.

FANCY FLIER

Connect the dots from **1** to **5**.
Color the picture.

SNEAKY SPIDER

Connect the dots from **1** to **5**.
Color the picture.

HAPPY HOUSE

Connect the dots from 1 to 5.
Color the picture.

CHEESE, PLEASE!

Connect the dots from **1** to **5**.
Color the picture.

WHO HOOTS?

Connect the dots from **1** to **5**.
Color the picture.

FLYING IS FUN!

Connect the dots from **1** to **5**.
Color the picture.

Connect the dots from **1** to **10**.
Color the picture.

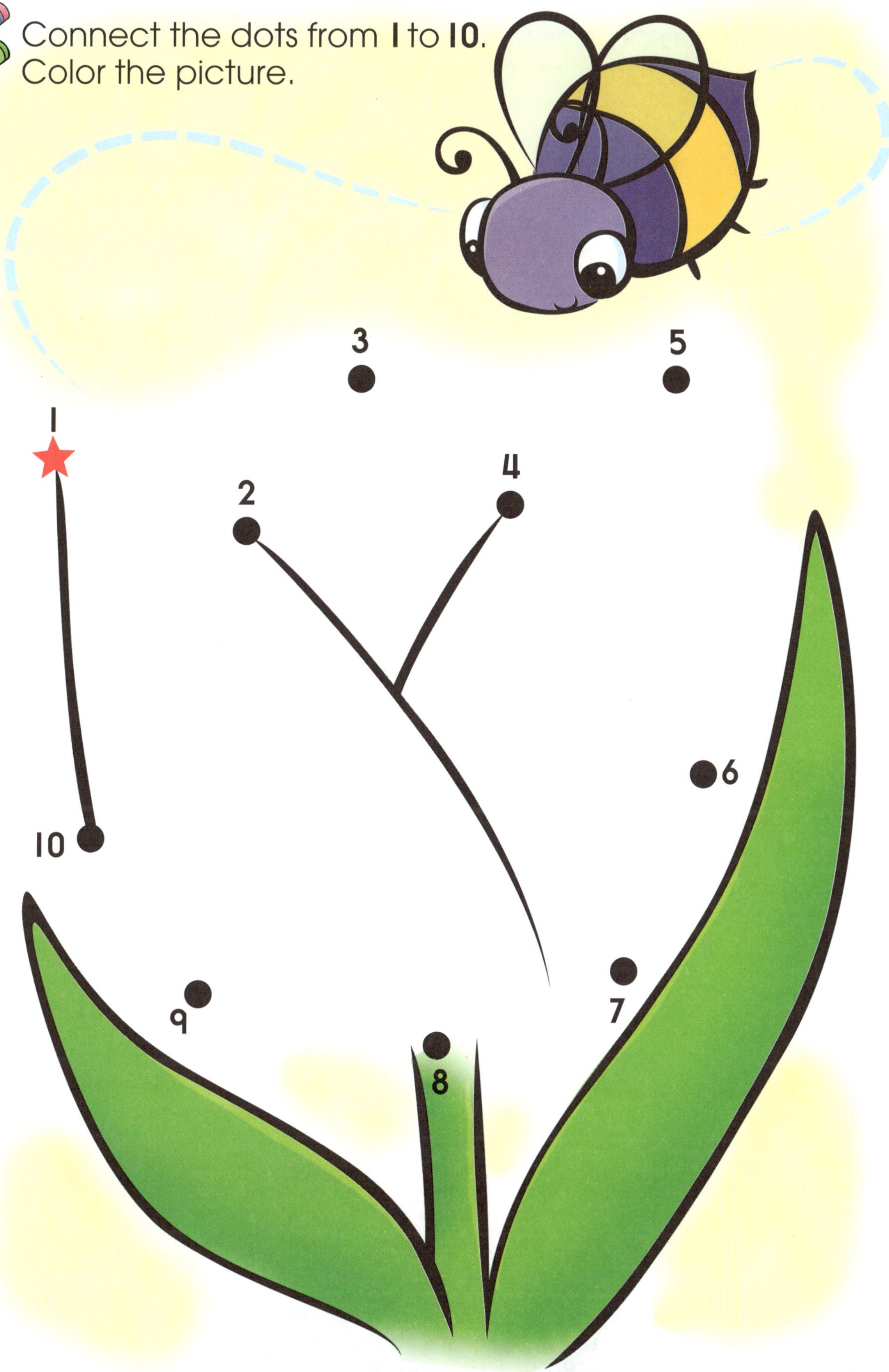

JUST CLUCKY

Connect the dots from 1 to 10.
Color the picture.

PURR-FECT PET

Connect the dots from **1** to **10**.
Color the picture.

AUTUMN ACORN

Connect the dots from **1** to **10**.
Color the picture.

COZY CABIN

Connect the dots from **1** to **10**.
Color the picture.

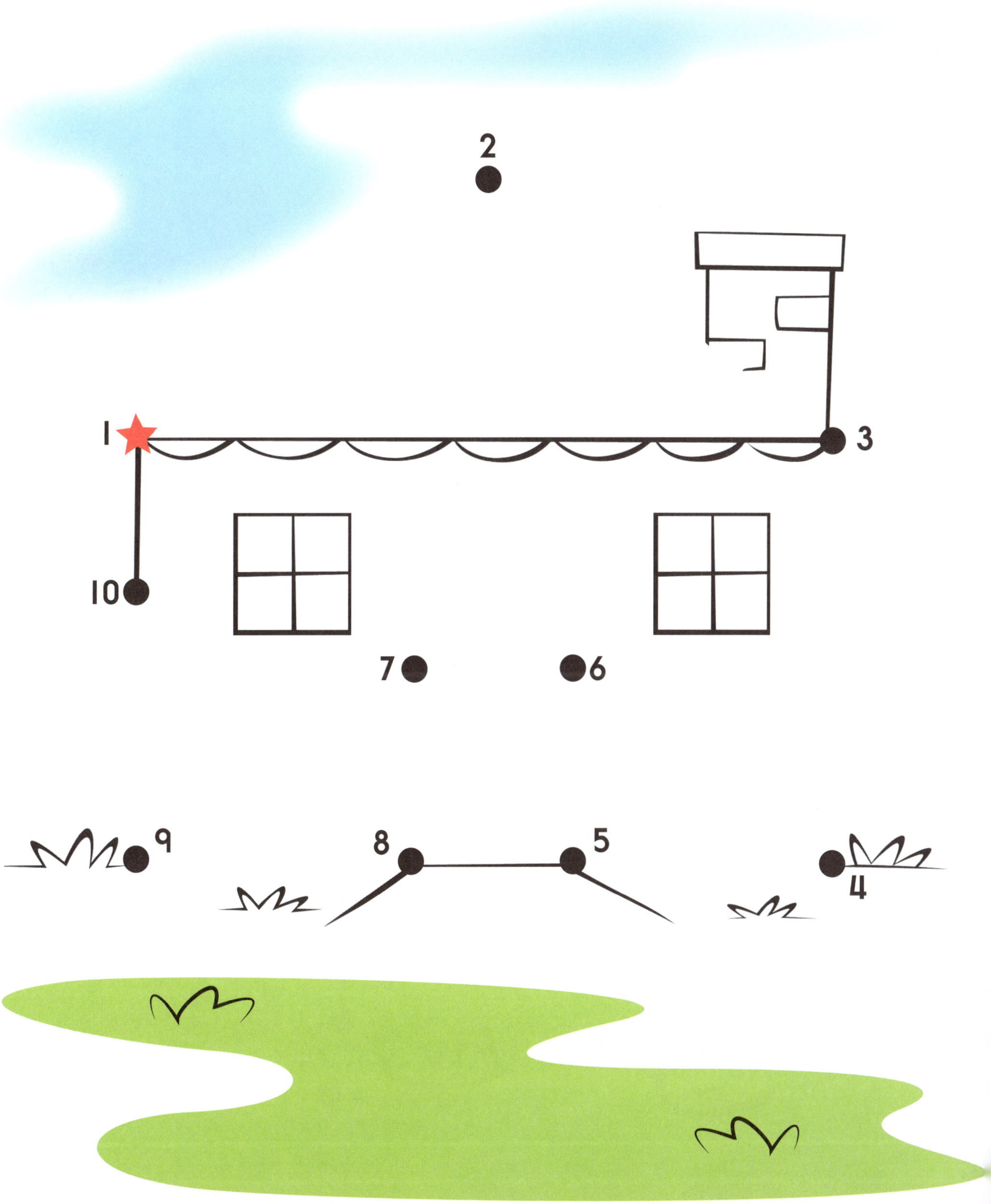

GENTLE GIANT

Connect the dots from 1 to 10.
Color the picture.

MISSY MOUSE

Connect the dots from **1** to **10**.
Color the picture.

FRIENDLY FISH

Connect the dots from **1** to **10**.
Color the picture.

SILLY SPACEMAN

Connect the dots from **1** to **15**.
Color the picture.

LITTLE LADY

Connect the dots from 1 to 15.
Color the picture.

PROUD PELICAN

Connect the dots from **1** to **15**.
Color the picture.

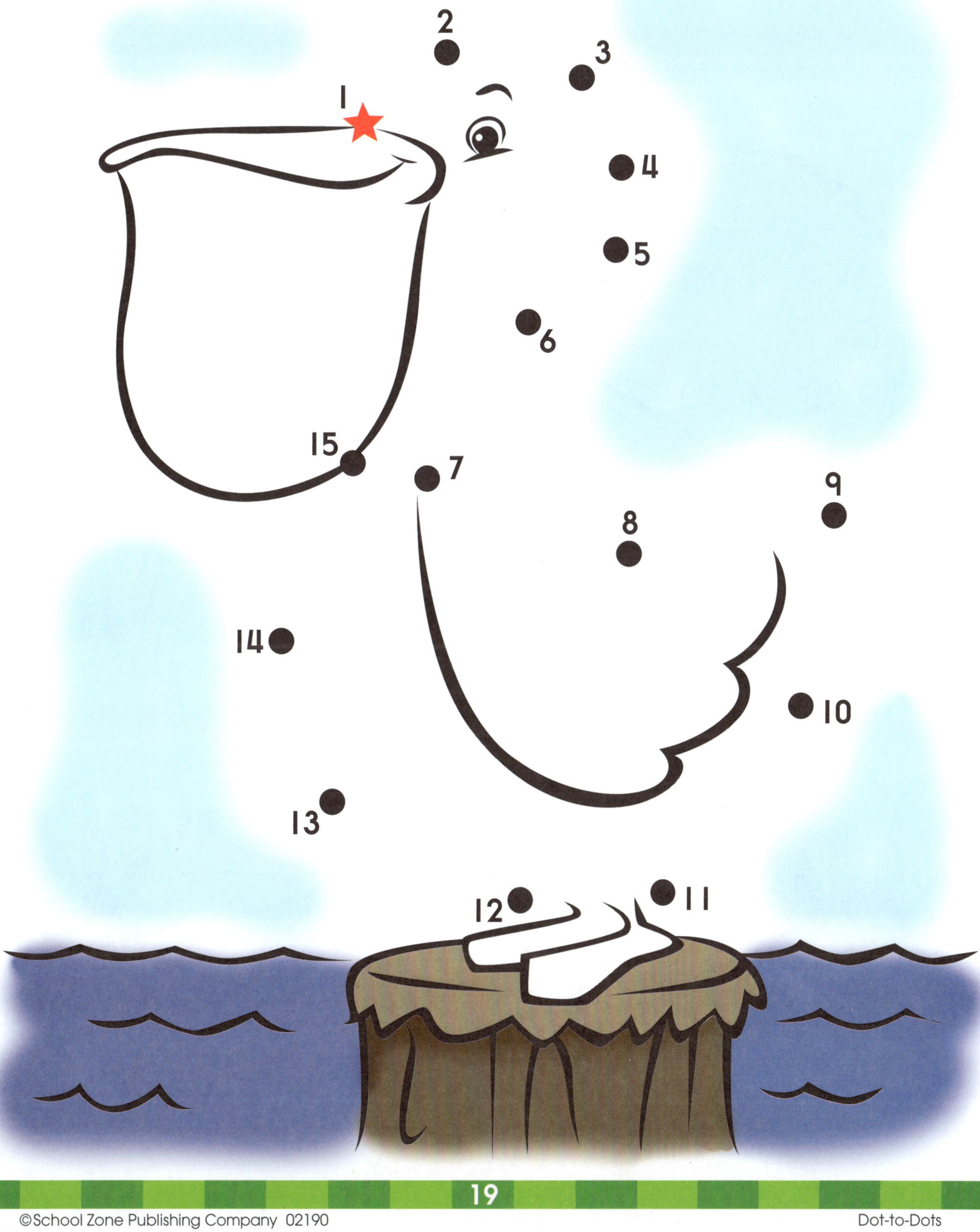

BUSY BEAVER

Connect the dots from **1** to **15**.
Color the picture.

ROWDY RHINO

Connect the dots from **1** to **15**.
Color the picture.

PLAYFUL POLAR BEAR

Connect the dots from **1** to **20**.
Color the picture.

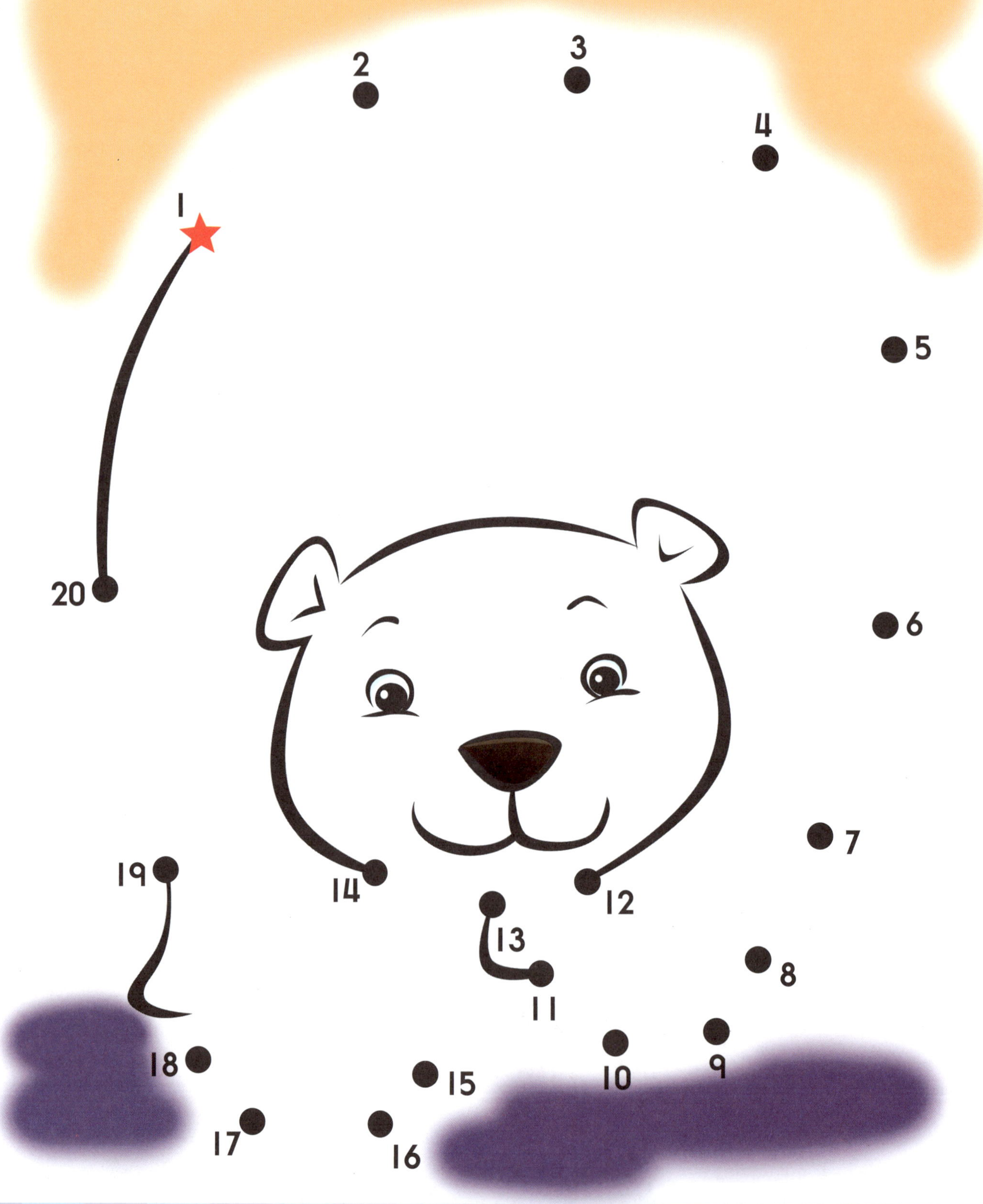

ROAMING RABBIT

Connect the dots from **1** to **20**.
Color the picture.

SWIMMING SWAN

Connect the dots from **1** to **20**.
Color the picture.

ROBBIE ROBOT

Connect the dots from **1** to **20**.
Color the picture.

PRANCING PENGUIN

Connect the dots from **1** to **20**.
Color the picture.

SETTING SAIL

Connect the dots from **1** to **25**.
Color the picture.

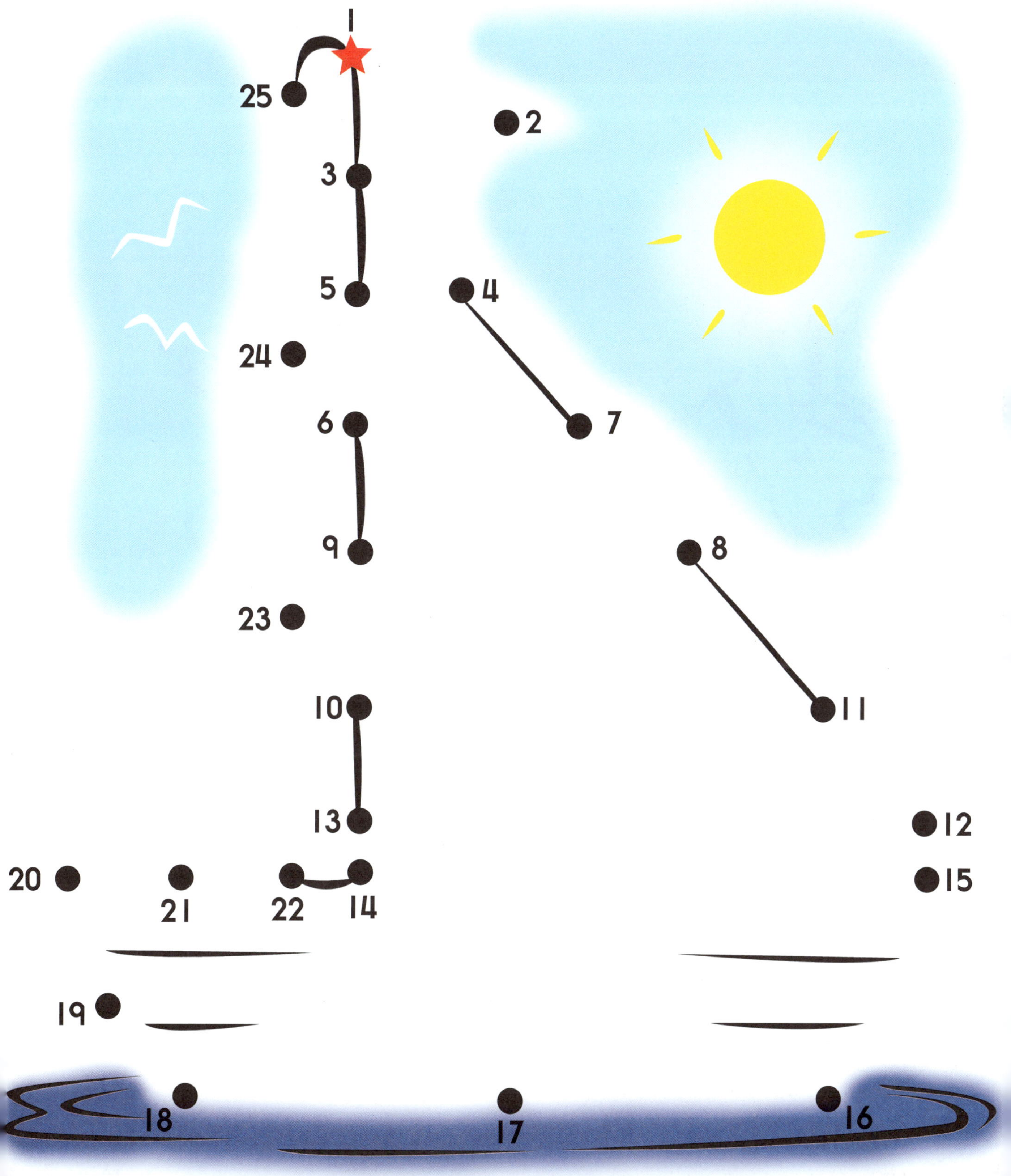

Connect the dots from **1** to **25**.
Color the picture.

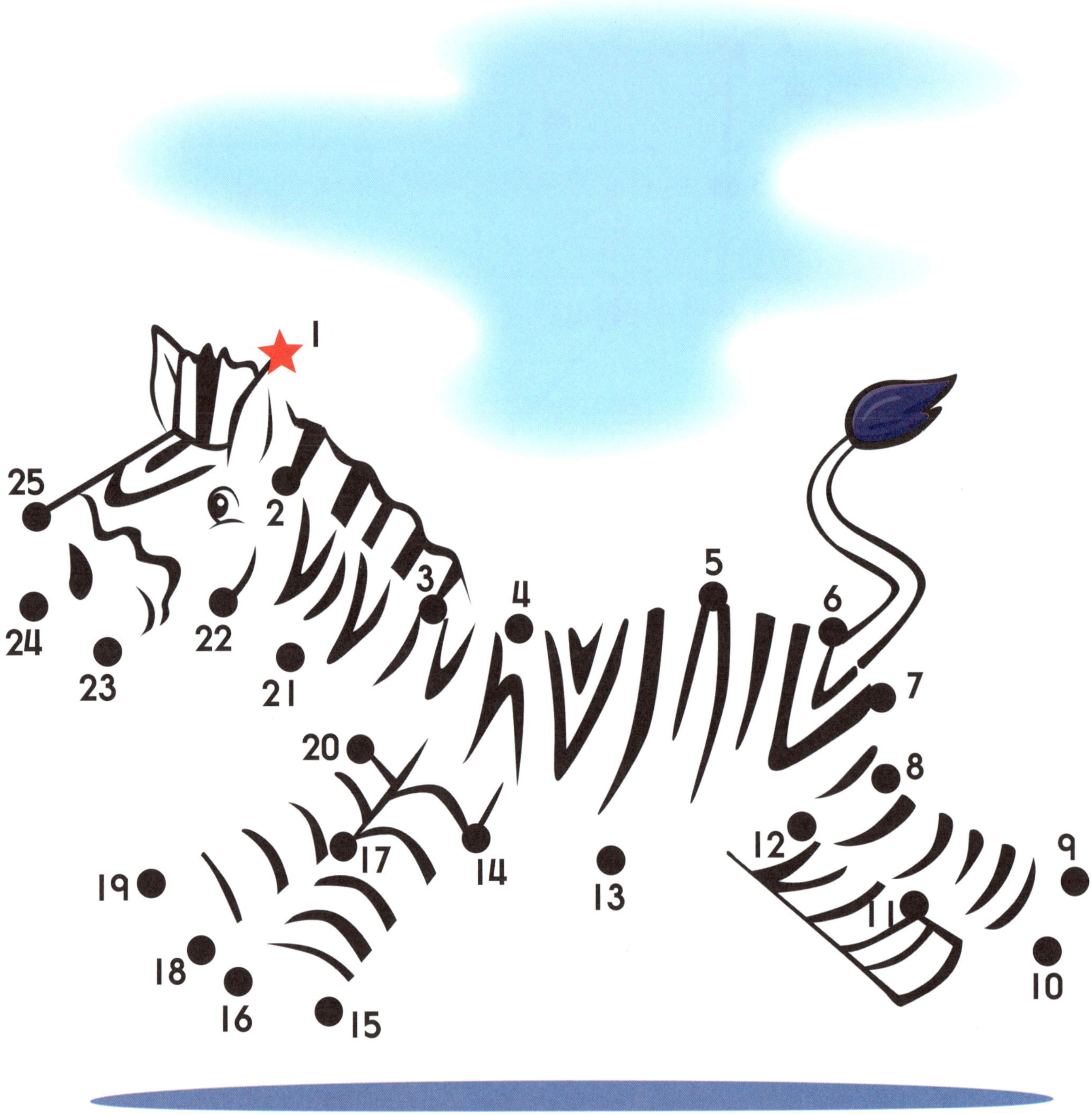

MOON MISSION

Connect the dots from **1** to **25**.
Color the picture.

RESTING RASCAL

Connect the dots from **1** to **25**.
Color the picture.

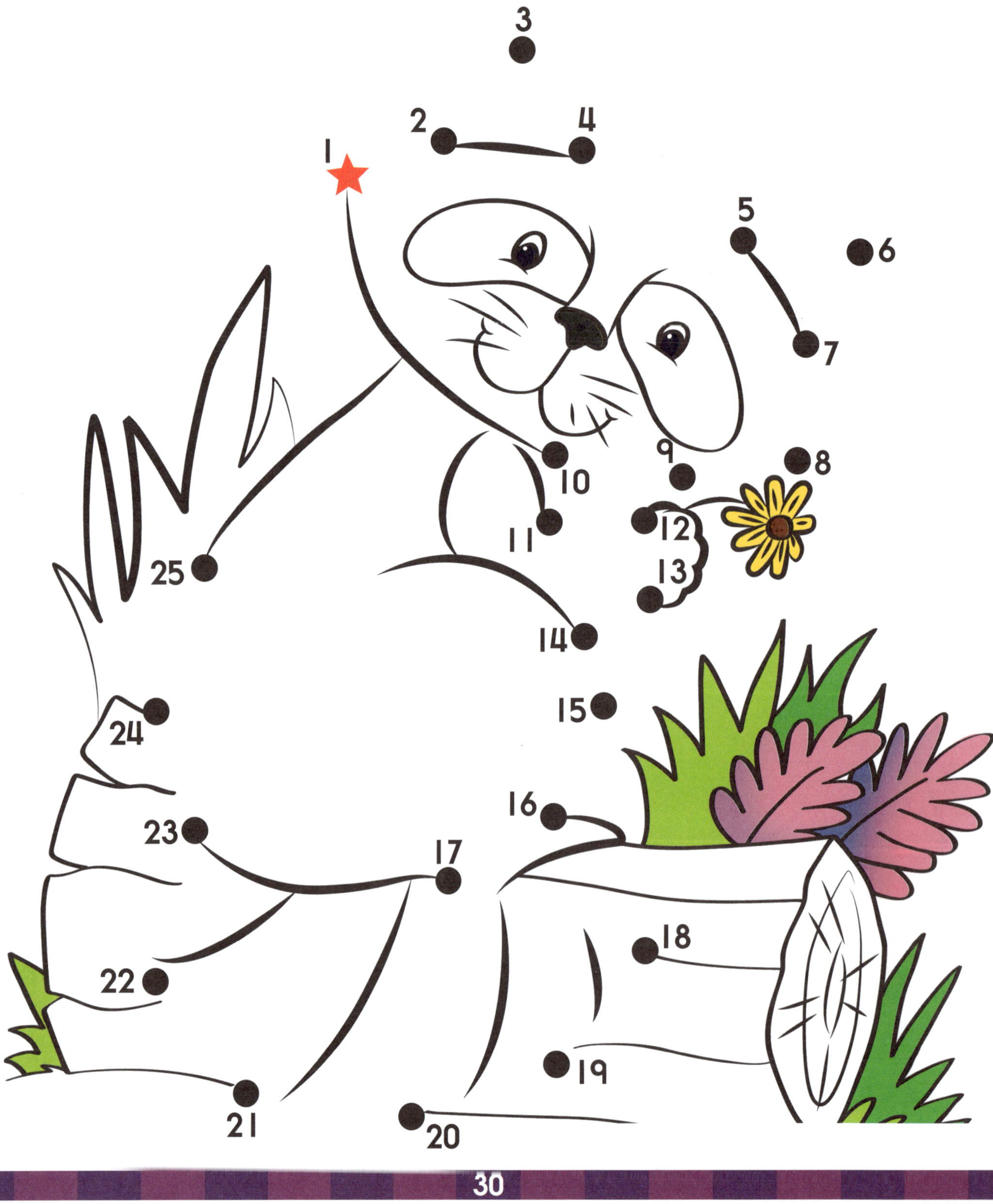

HOPPY HARE

Connect the dots from **1** to **25**.
Color the picture.

SOMETHING FISHY

Connect the dots from **1** to **25**.
Color the picture.

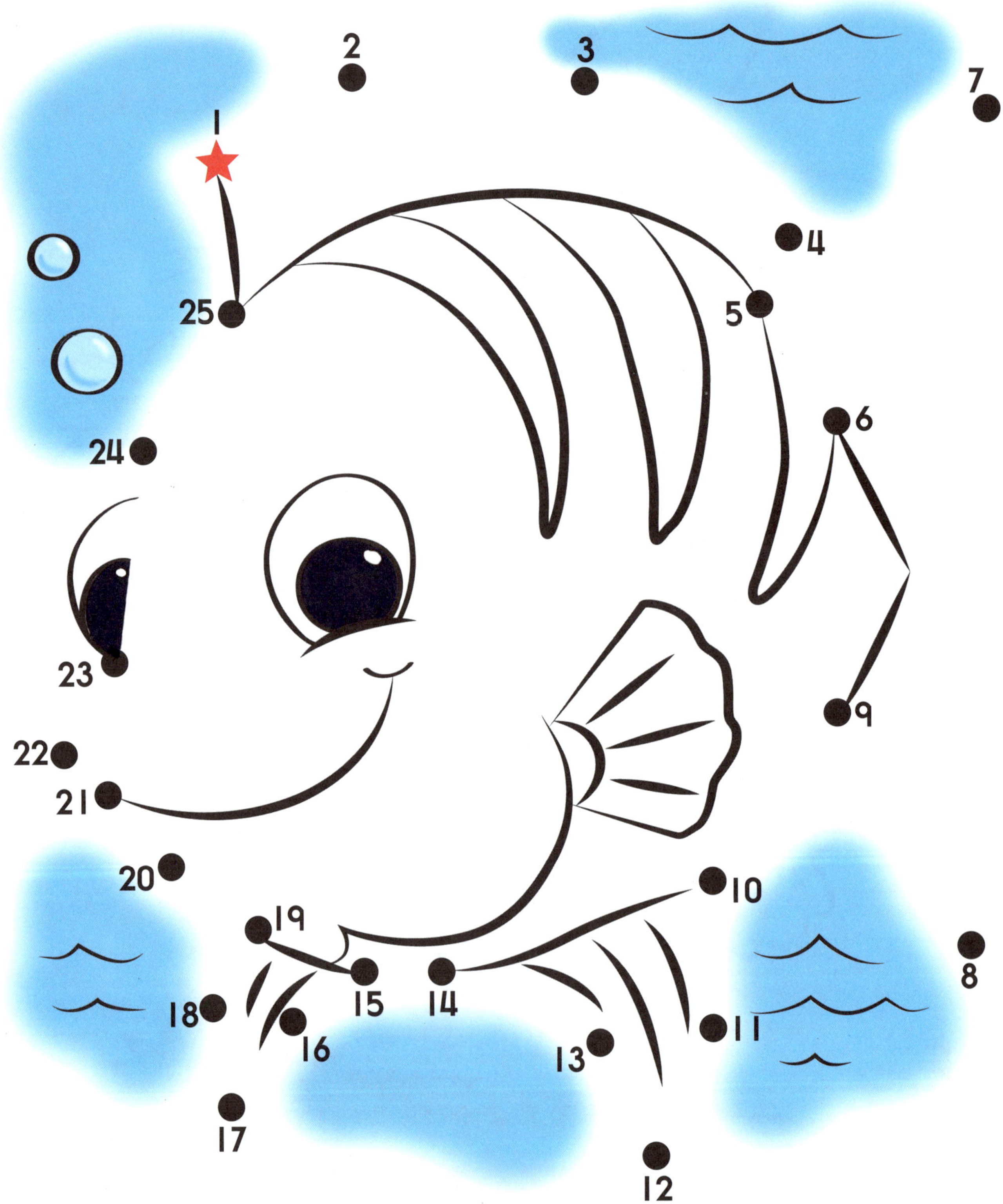